P9-ARP-776

Whale Sharks

by Nico Barnes

Visit us at www.abdopublishing.com

Published by Abdo Kids, a division of ABDO, PO Box 398166, Minneapolis, Minnesota 55439.

Copyright © 2015 by Abdo Consulting Group, Inc. International copyrights reserved in all countries. No part of this book may be reproduced in any form without written permission from the publisher.

Printed in the United States of America, North Mankato, Minnesota.

032014

092014

 PRINTED ON RECYCLED PAPER

Photo Credits: Getty Images, Glow Images, Minden Pictures, Shutterstock, Thinkstock

Production Contributors: Teddy Borth, Jennie Forsberg, Grace Hansen

Design Contributors: Dorothy Toth, Renée LaViolette, Laura Rask

Library of Congress Control Number: 2013952579

Cataloging-in-Publication Data

Barnes, Nico.

 Whale sharks / Nico Barnes.

  p. cm. -- (Sharks)

ISBN 978-1-62970-068-7 (lib. bdg.)

Includes bibliographical references and index.

1. Whale sharks--Juvenile literature. I. Title.

597.3--dc23

              2013952579

657 2240

Table of Contents

Whale Sharks

Whale sharks are the largest fish in the ocean!

Whale sharks **enjoy** warm ocean water. They are usually found near the **equator**.

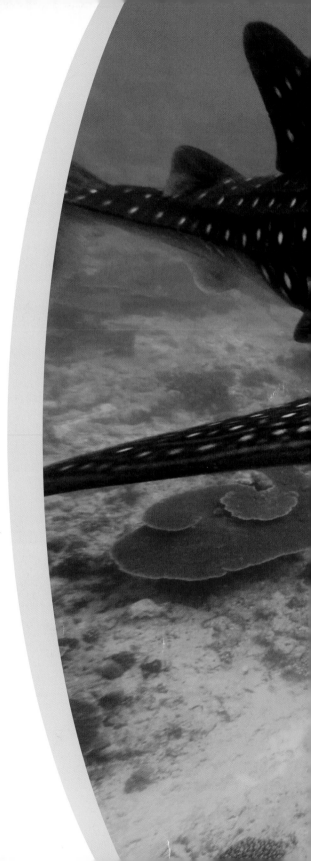

Whale sharks can be

brown, gray, or blue.

9

Whale sharks have spots and stripes. They have white bellies.

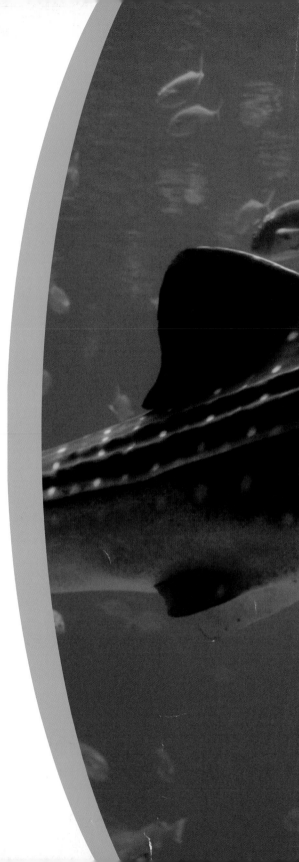

Like all sharks, whale sharks do not have bones. They are made of **cartilage**.

13

Food

Whale sharks have many rows of teeth. But they do not use their teeth to eat.

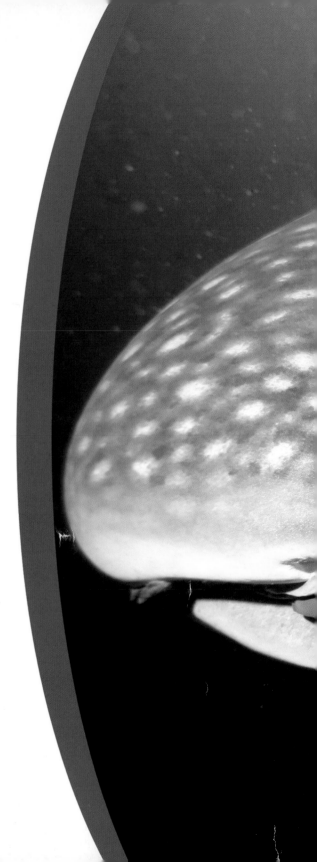

14

Whale sharks open their huge mouths to suck in water and food. They push the water out of their **gills** and swallow the food.

A whale shark's

favorite food is **krill**.

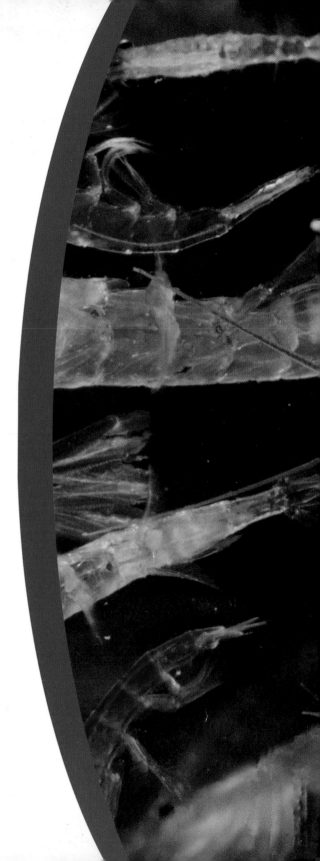

19

Baby Whale Sharks

Baby whale sharks are called **pups**. They are on their own once they are born.

More Facts

- Whale sharks are huge. They are about as long as a school bus. Some are even longer!

- Whale sharks move slowly. They only swim about 3 mph (5 kph).

- Whale sharks are harmless toward humans. Divers often swim with them.

Glossary

cartilage – matter that is tough and bendable. Your nose and ears are made out of cartilage.

enjoy – to find happiness in.

equator – an imaginary circle around the middle of the Earth. It splits the Earth into two equal parts.

gill – an organ that helps underwater animals breathe.

krill – small shrimplike animals of the open sea.

pup – a newborn animal.

Index

abdokids.com

Use this code to log on to abdokids.com and access crafts, games, videos and more!

Abdo Kids Code:
SWK0687

EMMA S. CLARK MEMORIAL LIBRARY

SETAUKET, NEW YORK 11733

To view your patron account,

renew or request an item,

visit www.emmaclark.org